Bible Stories for Children

Illustrated by

Janet & Anne Grahame Johnstone

Ideals Publishing Corp.

Milwaukee, Wisconsin

ISBN 0-8249-8017-4   325

Arrival in Bethlehem

MARY and Joseph lived in a small town called Nazareth. Joseph was a carpenter. Mary was expecting a baby. One day Joseph came in from his workshop with some news.

"We must go to Bethlehem. The Roman Emperor has ordered everyone to go to the town where he was born, to be taxed."

A week later, Mary and Joseph left their home to start on the long journey to Bethlehem. They travelled by donkey. The road was rough and the journey very uncomfortable. By the time they reached Bethlehem they were very tired.

They looked everywhere, trying to find a room for the night. All the hotels were full and nobody wanted them. At last they

persuaded an inn-
keeper to let
them sleep in
his stable.

The Birth of Jesus

THE stable was warm with the breath of the cattle. The floor was covered with hay and the donkeys and oxen stood quietly in their stalls. The innkeeper had given Joseph a candle which was standing on a stool in one corner. It sent soft shadows around the bare walls.

Mary knew that very soon the baby God had sent her would be born. What could she use for a cot? She looked around the stable. There, at the far end, was the manger from which normally the cattle ate. Mary decided to use it. She started to make a comfortable bed of the soft sweet hay.

Later that night, when all was very quiet except for the gentle sound of the wind among the trees, Mary's baby was born. He was a little boy and Mary called him Jesus, as God had told her. She had no clothes for him, so she wrapped him in a plain strip of material and laid him in the bed she had made in the manger.

The Shepherds

ON a hill outside Bethlehem some shepherds were minding their sheep. Suddenly an angel appeared telling them to go to the stable and find the baby Jesus. When they found him they knelt and worshipped him.

Adoration of the Magi

ON the evening when Jesus was born three clever and important men were talking together. One of them was standing gazing at the lovely starry sky. Suddenly he pointed to a star which was much brighter than the rest.

"That is the star we have been waiting for," he said.

The other two men were very excited.

"It's the star which tells us the baby Jesus has been born. We'll go and worship him."

They set off for the king's palace. They were sure that was where they would find Jesus. But when they got there the king said he knew nothing about the baby.

"If you find him come back and tell me," he said.

The three men went on their journey. The star led them all the way to the stable. Then it stopped.

"He can't be in there," said the men.

But they went in very quietly. Over in the corner a little light was shining. And there was the baby Jesus, with Mary and Joseph.

The three wise men knelt down and gave him the beautiful presents they had brought. Then they said a 'thank you' prayer to God because they knew that God had sent his son to tell people that he loved them.

Jesus in the Temple

ONE day, when Jesus was twelve years old, he rushed into his father's workshop.

"Father! We're nearly ready to leave!"

His parents were taking him to the Festival at Jerusalem. They were travelling with a group of friends and relations.

Never had Jesus seen so many people as there were when they arrived in Jerusalem. He had so many questions to ask, and so much to talk about that the time went much too quickly. His parents smiled at his excitement. But when it was time to go home they could not find him.

"He must be with the other children," they said, as the donkeys moved forward.

But that night they discovered he was not in the group at all.

"We must go back and look for him," said Mary.

So Mary and Joseph went back to Jerusalem. They looked everywhere but could not find him.

"Let's go to the Temple and ask if anyone has seen him," said Mary.

When they went into the temple they were very surprised. Jesus was sitting quite happily talking to the priests.

"Why didn't you stay with us?" asked Mary. "We have looked for you everywhere."

"Didn't you know you would find me in God's house? I have work to do for him," Jesus answered. "But I'm ready now."

And he went back to Nazareth with Joseph and Mary.

The Sower and the Seed

JESUS used to explain things to people by telling them stories. Sometimes it seemed as though they never would understand what he was trying to teach them.

One day, when he was teaching the people that they ought to listen to God and do what he asked them to do, he told them this story:

A sower went out into a field to sow some seed. As he walked along he scattered the seed first to the right and then to the left and it fell on to the ground around him. Some of it fell on the path where there was no earth, and it could not grow. But it did not stay there for long because the birds flew down and ate it.

"This," explained Jesus, "is like the people who don't listen to God when he speaks to them."

Then some of the seed fell on to the stony ground, where it began to grow. But it had no roots and when the sun came out the little shoots were so weak that they withered away and died.

"This," Jesus said, "is like the people who listen to what God tells them but soon forget all that he says."

Some seed fell into the brambles. When it began to grow the thorns of the brambles got in the way and choked the plants so that they, too, began to die. This is like the people who listen to God and intend to do as he tells them, but soon money and earthly possessions become more important to them.

"But," said Jesus, "a lot of the seed fell on to good earth and it grew until it was very tall. It waved in the breeze like a golden sea. As the sower looked at it he knew that although he had sown it, it had been God's rain and sun on the good earth that had made it so beautiful. These seeds are like the people who listen to God and do as he tells them."

The Woman with the Piece of Silver

ONCE Jesus told a story to explain to everyone how much God loves them.

God is always ready to forgive his people, and he will go on loving and forgiving them even when they don't love him.

Once there was a woman who owned ten silver pieces of money. Each one was worth a great deal and she tried to keep them very safe. One day one of the pieces was missing. She was very worried and began to look for it. She looked in the room where the money was kept. She searched under all the furniture. No, it was not under any of the things in that room.

"Perhaps it has rolled into one of the dark corners where I

cannot see it shine," the woman said.

So she looked in all the corners in the hope of finding the precious piece of silver. But it was not anywhere in that room. She searched in the next room and the next, but still she could not find the money.

"What shall I do?" she said. "Perhaps some of my friends and neighbours will help me find it."

She went to tell her friends about it.

"Of course we'll come and help you," they said. "But why bother so much about one? You still have nine pieces."

"I won't be really happy until I have them all," she replied.

They went to the woman's home. Some searched the house, while others went outside and looked for the money in the courtyard and on the road. It was nearly dark when they returned and still the money had not been found. The woman was very unhappy but she thanked her friends for helping.

"It may be I shall find it, even now," she said. Her friends started on their way home and she went back into the house.

She lit a candle. It sent wavering shadows around the room. As she went towards the door something on the floor caught her eye. It shone brilliantly in the light. The woman bent down and there was the piece of silver for which she had been looking. She picked it up and ran down the road after her friends.

"Look!" she said. "I have found the silver!"

"We are pleased," they said. "We thought you would find it in the end."

The Miraculous Catch of Fishes

ONE day Jesus borrowed his disciple Peter's boat. He taught the people from it, for there was a great crowd listening to Him from the shore.

When he had finished teaching, Jesus said:

"Launch out into the deep water and let down your net."

Peter told Jesus that they had fished all night and caught nothing.

"But," said Peter, "at your word, I will let down my net."

And when they had let down their net Peter and his brother

Andrew pulled it in again. It was so full of fish and so heavy that the net broke.

Then Peter and Andrew had to call to James and John and their friends to help them bring their great catch of fish to the shore.

Feeding the Five Thousand

AFTER these things had happened people began to follow Jesus everywhere.

One day, when he wanted to talk quietly to his disciples, he took them right away from the town to a place where they could be alone. But there were many people who wanted to hear what Jesus had to say, and soon they found out where he had gone and followed him. Now, instead of there being just Jesus and the twelve disciples, there were Jesus, the twelve disciples, and a great crowd of people.

Time passed quickly as Jesus talked. Everybody was so interested that they stayed on and on, until at last they were very hungry.

The disciples came to Jesus to ask if they should send the people home.

"Give them something to eat first," said Jesus.

The disciples looked at Jesus in astonishment.

"We haven't the food or the money," they said. "It would cost a lot to feed all these people."

A boy who was standing near, heard the disciple talking about food. He thought of the basket beside him which his mother had packed before he left home. There was not much in it. Just five barley cakes and two small fishes; only enough for him. But if Jesus needed them he would not keep them for himself.

He plucked up his courage and tugged at the sleeve of the disciple nearest to him. When the disciple looked down at him the boy was glad to see that it was Andrew, who was always friendly.

"What is it, son?" asked Andrew.

"I've got some cakes and fishes here," he said. "You could give those to Jesus and he could share them out among the people. It's not very much, but if Jesus had it there might be enough for some."

Andrew laughed as he looked into the basket.

"It won't go very far among this crowd," he said.

"Take it to Jesus and see," said the boy.

So Andrew took the basket to Jesus and said:

"There's a boy who says you can have his cakes and fishes."

"Thank you," said Jesus.

Then he turned to his disciples and said:

"Tell the people to sit down."

When Jesus had blessed the food he broke the cakes into pieces and divided the fishes. Then he called the disciples and told them to take the food round to the people. There was something for everyone, and they all ate until they were satisfied.

"Take these baskets and collect the pieces which are left," said Jesus to his disciples.

Each of the disciples took a basket and filled it with the pieces. When they returned to Jesus they were amazed to see that every basket was full.

The Good Samaritan

A certain lawyer came to Jesus and asked Him,
"What must I do to go to heaven?"
Jesus answered:
"Love God with all your heart and mind, and love your neighbour as much as yourself."
The lawyer said:
"Who is my neighbour?"
Then Jesus told this story.

"A man was travelling to a town called Jericho. On the way robbers attacked him. They stole everything he had, took his clothes, wounded him badly and left him lying, half dead, by the road.

Later a priest passed by, but he left the poor traveller lying there and crossed to the other side of the road.

Then a Levite, a man who helped in the temple, came by. He too crossed over and did not help the poor wounded traveller.

The third man to pass was a Samaritan.

The Jews and the Samaritans were not friends and the people listening expected Jesus to say that the Samaritan would be hard-hearted too.

But Jesus continued:

"The Samaritan stopped. He picked up the poor man and tended his wounds with oil and wine to make the wounds heal. He put some of his own clothes on the traveller and took him on his donkey to an inn.

At the inn the Samaritan paid for the wounded man to be looked after. He promised he would come back and pay any more money that was owing."

Then Jesus asked the lawyer and the people listening:

"Which of all these men do you think was a neighbour to the man the robbers hurt?"
The lawyer replied:
"The Samaritan that helped him."
Jesus said:
"You must do the same for your neighbours."

The Lost Sheep

IN spite of all the things Jesus taught them, the Pharisees and leaders of the people either could not or would not understand how great is God's love. They still thought that Jesus ought not to have anything to do with the tax gatherers and others who did things which were wrong.

"Look at him," they said, when they saw him attracting such people. "He's letting all those wicked people follow him around. He ought to have nothing to do with them."

"He encourages them," said another man. "He even went to have supper with some of them the other night. That's a thing we would never do."

Jesus heard them grumbling among themselves about him.

"God's love reaches out to everyone," he said. "I'll tell you a story which will help you to understand this.

"There was once a shepherd who had a hundred sheep. Every day he took them out on the fields and hillsides and let them roam and look for fresh grass. Mostly they kept together as sheep do. Then one of them became a little venturesome. She wandered away from the rest of the flock looking for more tasty pieces of grass and scrub. Then, still further away, she saw some which looked even better. She wandered on and on not noticing where she was going until she was so far away from the rest of the flock that she could not see or hear them.

"At the end of the day the shepherd came to take his sheep home. He counted them one by one as they went into the fold. There were only ninety-nine. One of them was missing.

"Now," said Jesus, "what would you have done if it had been your sheep that was missing? Would you have let her stay lost?"

The people who were listening knew they would not do any such thing. Each one of the sheep would be valuable to them, and they began to understand why Jesus was telling them this story. But they said nothing, so Jesus answered his own question.